My First Time
Getting Ready to Move

by Jeri Cipriano

Red Chair Press   Egremont, Massachusetts

Look! Books are produced and published by Red Chair Press:

Red Chair Press LLC   PO Box 333   South Egremont, MA 01258-0333

 FREE Educator Guides at www.redchairpress.com/free-resources

Publisher's Cataloging-In-Publication Data

Names: Cipriano, Jeri, author.

Title: Getting ready to move / by Jeri Cipriano.

Description: Egremont, Massachusetts : Red Chair Press, [2021] | Series: Look! books. My first time | Includes index and a list of resources for further reading. | Interest age level: 005-008. | Summary: "When a parent gets a new job, often the family must move to a new city. Sometimes, people move across town to a new house. But in either case moving can be scary. Giving up your neighborhood friends, the bedroom you know, maybe moving to a new school. Saying goodbye is hard, but meeting new friends is exciting. Discover what you need to know about getting ready to move"--Provided by publisher.

Identifiers: ISBN 9781643710952 (RLB hardcover) | ISBN 9781643711010 (softcover) | ISBN 9781643711072 (ebook)

Subjects: LCSH: Moving, Household--Juvenile literature. | Moving, Household--Psychological aspects--Juvenile literature. | CYAC: Moving, Household. | Moving, Household--Psychological aspects.

Classification: LCC TX307 .C56 2021 (print) | LCC TX307 (ebook) | DDC 648.9--dc23

LCCN: 2020948762

Photo credits: iStock

Printed in United States of America
0421 1P   CGF21

Table of Contents

Making Changes

Change is all around us. Seasons change. Leaves change colors. Puppies grow into dogs.

You change too. You grow taller each year. Baby teeth fall out and new teeth come in.

Everyone makes changes. See the changes below. How many changes have you made?

- You moved to where you live now.
- You changed schools.
- You changed grades and got a new teacher.
- You got a new pet.
- You got a new baby sister or brother.
- You went from a beginner bike to a two-wheeler.

If you made one or two of the changes above, take a bow.

Things change all the time.
We change every day.

Moving

For most children, **moving** to a new place is a big change. They know where they are. But they don't know what living in a new place will be like.

"Not knowing" makes moving scary. Feelings go up and down like a roller coaster. One day you are mad. The next day you are sad. Sometimes you even feel glad.

If you are moving, you will have many feelings. Tell people how you feel. Friends and family can help you feel better.

This book will help, too.

Where Are You Going?

Knowing where you are going takes away many worries.

If you can, make a car trip. Drive around your **neighborhood**. Find your school. Find a playground or park. Spend the day.

Good to Know

Take pictures of places that interest you. They will look familiar when you move in. Write down what you see. Write how you feel about each place.

If possible, visit your new neighborhood with your family before your move.

Make an Online Visit

If you are moving far, you and your family can visit **online**. Let Google Maps take you to your new house and neighborhood.

Good to Know

Look for your new school. Find the school **website**. Read about the school. How do the children look? What things are they doing? Have your family show you the way you will travel to school.

Getting Ready

Stick to your regular routines, like normal bedtime. But make time to help fill boxes with your things, like clothes and toys. Leave out what you will carry with you, like a favorite stuffed animal.

Think Ahead

Know where your room will be.
How do you want it to look?
What color paint will you choose?
Where will you put your things?

Fill a Memory Box

Cover a shoe box with paper. Decorate the box with colored markers and stickers. Fill your box with keepsakes, such as photos of friends and notes from teachers.

Saying Goodbye

Spend time with people who are special. Visit places you want to remember. Take pictures or videos with friends. Trade addresses and phone numbers.

Before the move...
Call your new school and
ask for a "buddy pen pal"—
someone you can get to know
before moving.

After the move...
You can call your friends. You
can have a video call through
FaceTime or *Skype*.

Welcome the New

With a grown-up, walk around your new neighborhood. Make **"eye contact"** with children your age. Smile. A "smile" is a great way of sending a message. A smile says "I am friendly. How about you?"

Good to Know

Contact your new school. Ask the principal to introduce you to a few children. Have your family plan play dates with their families.

Getting Comfortable

Unpacking is a lot of work. Make time for fun. Prepare a "welcome" gift for your family. Play a game. Laugh. Laughing helps everyone relax.

Just Remember: *Home* is where the people you love are. When you move, you are always "at home."

22

Words to Know

eye contact: looking into another's eyes

move: a change of place to live

neighborhood: the area surrounding your house

online: making a computer connection

website: a place connected to the Internet

Learn More at the Library

Check out these books to learn more.

Blackaby, Susan. *Moving Day.* Picture Window Books, 2005.

Nelson, Maria. *I Am a Good Neighbor.* Gareth Stevens, 2013.

Rober, Harold T. *Moving Day.* Lerner Publishing, 2017.

Index

About the Author

Jeri Cipriano enjoys writing for children of all ages. She loves to learn new things she can share with others.